SPEED RACERS

RACING PERSONAL WATERCRAFT
(SEA-DOOS)

Jill Sherman

Enslow Publishing
101 W. 23rd Street
Suite 240
New York, NY 10011
USA

enslow.com

Published in 2018 by Enslow Publishing, LLC.
101 W. 23rd Street, Suite 240, New York, NY 10011

Library of Congress Cataloging-in-Publication Data
Names: Sherman, Jill, author.
Title: Racing personal watercraft (Sea-doos) / Jill Sherman.
Description: New York : Enslow Publishing, 2018. | Series: Speed racers |
  Includes bibliographical references and index.
Identifiers: LCCN 2017022694| ISBN 9780766092716 (library bound) | ISBN
  9780766094222 (pbk.) | ISBN 9780766094239 (6 pack)
Subjects: LCSH: Personal watercraft racing—Juvenile literature.
Classification: LCC GV835.94 .S54 2018 | DDC 797.3—dc23
LC record available at https://lccn.loc.gov/2017022694

Printed in the United States of America

To Our Readers: We have done our best to make sure all websites in
this book were active and appropriate when we went to press. However,
the author and the publisher have no control over and assume no
liability for the material available on those websites or on any websites
they may link to. Any comments or suggestions can be sent by email to
customerservice@enslow.com.

Photo Credits: Cover, p. 1 bondvit/Shutterstock.com; pp. 4, 7
Karim Jaafar/AFP/Getty Images; p. 5 Ahmed Adly/Shutterstock.com; pp.
8, 13 crokogen/iStockphoto.com; p. 9 Kidsixteen/Wikimedia Commons/
Cj2 wiki3.jpg/public domain; p. 11 ManoAfrica/iStockphoto.com; pp. 14,
17, 20 ChuckSchugPhotography/iStockphoto.com; p. 18 Photoservice/
iStockphoto.com; p. 24 Anton Novoderezhkin/TASS/Getty Images;
pp. 27, 30 sewer11/iStockphoto.com; pp. 28, 34 grahamheywood/
iStockphoto.com; pp. 33, 36 gsermek/iStockphoto.com; pp. 39, 42
Kimbra Ritchie/iStockphoto.com; p. 41 Charles Schug/iStockphoto.com.

▶ Contents

Let's Ride!

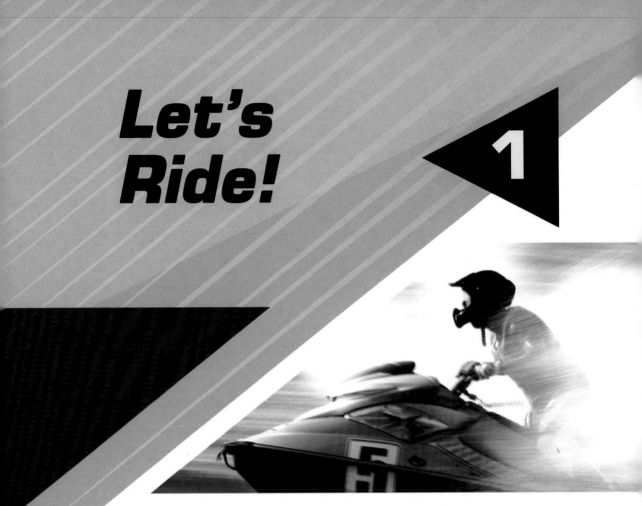

1

E rminio Iantosca pulled his Sea-Doo up to the starting line. He looked around at the racers beside him. They had all qualified to be here. They were the best that the sport had to offer. But today, they were putting it all on the line. It was the 2016 Pro Watercross World Championships. Only one of the racers would walk away with the championship prize.

The annual race takes place in Naples, Florida, Iantosca's home town. After a disappointing race the year before, Iantosca was determined to make his fans proud. "I've got a lot better

When racers line up at the start line, they get ready to open their throttles.

equipment (this year)," he said. "I've been testing the past month. I'm confident. I'm not going to get fifth this year." Iantosca races in the Pro Runabout GP class. "GP" means there are no rules on the modifications or upgrades that racers can make to their watercraft.

But Iantosca knows this race is just as much about his skill. When the signal goes off, Iantosca opens up the throttle. Riders zoom out from the starting line. Water sprays up behind them. Rocketing toward the buoys, racers navigate the course laid out for them. Because they're on the water, no inch of the course is the same. And waves from the surrounding boats make the water even choppier.

Luckily, Iantosca thrives on choppy water. His watercraft bounces across the water at top speed. He zips around buoy after buoy. He is in the lead. When he crosses the finish line, he is elated. Iantosca won the gold!

Need for Speed

Once you ride a personal watercraft (PWC), the urge to race is hard to resist. Organized races have a lot to offer. For the World Championships, "It's closed-course racing, similar to motocross on water," said Nick Handler, managing director of Pro Watercross. "There are left turns, right turns, and front and back straightaways. There are eighteen to twenty guys on the starting line, and they race around the course [for] a set number of laps."

At a big event like the World Championships, hundreds of riders will be there to compete. Riders are separated by the type of PWC they ride. Stock riders compete using their PWC as it comes from the manufacturer. They do not make modifications. Riders like Iantosca, on the other hand, soup up their rides to reach top speeds.

In addition to the races, freestyle riders compete by doing tricks. "(Riders) will be doing back flips, barrel rolls, 360 spins," Handler said. "It's definitely an attention-grabber. It's pretty cool for the fans."

Heart of a Racer

World Champion rider Erminio Iantosca got into riding when his father brought home a stand-up watercraft. Though he was too young to ride at the time, Iantosca was enthralled. Once he started riding, he practiced constantly.

He remembers his first race. "It was so cold, and I was just a little fourteen-year-old kid racing against twenty-four-year-old grown men in Novice Sport. And I went out there and won every race that day, and there was no turning back. I knew this was something I was going to do for a long time."

Souped-up PWCs reach top speeds on the water.

Riding Your Personal Watercraft

2

The idea for the personal watercraft began in the 1960s. Clayton Jacobson II was a motocross enthusiast. Racing off-road motorcycles was great. But Jacobson wanted to bring the thrill of motocross to the water. He began working on a stand-up watercraft.

Meanwhile, Laurent Beaudoin dreamed of doing the same thing. He worked for Bombardier, the maker of the Ski-Doo snowmobile. He thought that the Ski-Doo could be adapted to a watercraft. Beaudoin hired Jacobson to build his seated Sea-Doo.

Clayton Jacobson II (number 597) was an avid motocross racer. He is credited as the inventor of the PWC.

Later, Jacobson returned to building his stand-up craft. It would become Kawasaki's Jet Ski, first sold in 1973. It had a powerful 400cc engine and handlebar steering. The craft allowed riders to essentially waterski without the need for a motorboat.

However, these early PWCs were a challenge to use. Riders had a hard time staying upright, especially in choppy water. The Jet Ski managed to attract some loyal followers. The Sea-Doo, however, was not very popular. Sales were poor, so the company stopped making them.

But throughout the 1980s and 1990s, PWCs saw a number of improvements. They grew more stable, and new technology made PWCs easier to use. Soon, the Sea-Doo became the best-selling boat in the world.

Today's PWCs can carry up to three people at a time. They can reach speeds of 60 miles per hour (96 km/h). Riders can modify their PWCs to help them move even faster. The thrill of riding PWCs at high speeds has inspired many riders to race PWCs. The sport is popular in towns across the United States.

Riding a PWC

When you get on a PWC for the first time, it is important to know all the controls. To operate a PWC, you must first attach your safety lanyard. The PWC will not run without it. One end attaches to the PWC, and the other goes around your wrist. If you fall off of your PWC while riding, the lanyard will come unplugged, and the PWC will stop. Without the safety lanyard, the PWC would keep going, stranding you in the water. It could even crash into other boats.

You control a PWC's steering with the handlebars. This is also where you find the throttle. The throttle opens the water pump underneath the craft. A PWC works by sucking in water from below and shooting it out the back. The force of the water's motion moves the craft. Using the

Familiarize yourself with the PWC controls before taking your vehicle out on the water.

throttle, you can control how much water is pumped through your PWC. More water means more speed.

Remember, there are no brakes on the water. You need to avoid other objects on the water by applying the throttle and turning away from them. Once you let go of the throttle, you lose the ability to steer. Give yourself plenty of space to make a turn. If you are going at top speed, it can take 200 feet (61 m) or more to come to a complete stop. That is why it is important to go slowly while you are learning to ride a PWC. Once you get comfortable, you can start picking up speed. Some PWCs have the ability to move backward. You can use this to slow down if you need to avoid a collision.

Like driving a car, responsible riding means knowing the rules of the road. On the water, there are no actual roads. Boats, swimmers, birds, and other PWCs may be in any direction. You must stay alert at all times. It is your responsibility to get out of their way. Never assume that another boat will turn to avoid you.

Safety First

- Check your state's age limit. Manufacturers recommend that operators be at least sixteen years old. However, laws vary from state to state.
- Attach yourself to the vehicle's emergency engine cutoff lanyard.
- Always wear a life jacket.
- Stay out of shallow water.
- Stay at least 100 feet (30.5 m) from other boats.
- Stay at least 150 feet (45.7 m) from the shore or docks.
- Do not weave through boat traffic.

Lean forward to keep the PWC settled on the water.

With so many PWCs to choose from, take your time to find the right one for you.

Improving Your Technique

Operating a PWC is relatively simple—but controlling it takes practice. Many first-time riders will find themselves struggling to control their PWC. Much of this can be learned with proper weight placement.

One common riding error is called "porpoising." This is a leaping and surging of the PWC. When riders do this, it may feel like they are riding a bucking bronco at a rodeo. This happens when they open the throttle too hard. But rather than just trying to hold on, riders should learn to tame their rides. Most of the time, the problem is with the rider's position. If most of the rider's weight is to the rear, the PWC's nose will lift. Position your weight forward. Lean into the handlebars. Then set your feet farther back in the foot wells. You will be able to feel when the PWC is balanced.

Learning to make proper turns can be tricky. And for those who want to race watercross, good turning technique is essential. But when you make hard turns, you may find yourself sliding out of your seat. Leaning into a turn may feel right. But this is a habit you will have to break. When you carve the boat into a turn, you actually want to lean to the outside of your craft. Doing so takes a good amount of upper-body strength, so be prepared. It may be difficult to get used to, but it's well worth the effort. This technique will help you avoid going for an unexpected swim!

Once you have a handle on the basics, keep on riding. Practice, practice, practice. Learning the basics can be done in an afternoon, but it takes a lot of riding to become a pro.

Choosing Your Ride

Most riders start by renting a PWC while they are on vacation. Others may have friends with PWCs that they can ride. But if you're serious about racing, you will need your own PWC. Finding the right PWC for you depends on a few different factors.

First, consider the body of water where you'll do most of your riding. What are the typical conditions there? If you'll be riding on the ocean, the water may frequently get choppy. You probably won't want a small PWC, which will get tossed around on the waves. Smaller rides are better to use on calmer waters, like lakes or bays.

Superchargers can make a big difference in the speed of your craft. But they may not be great if you also want to use your PWC for recreation. They also use a lot of gas. Consider all your needs before going all out on a supercharger for your PWC.

Also, remember that you will have to tow your PWC to and from the water. Be sure when you choose your PWC that it is not too large for your car to manage.

The right PWC makes all the difference. Be sure to choose one that suits all your needs. Now, it's off to the races!

3 ▶ *Get Ready to Race*

Racing PWCs can be great fun. There are three types of races to consider when you are starting out: closed course, endurance racing, and drag racing.

Closed course is the most popular kind of PWC race. These races are similar to motocross races but are on the water. They are often called watercross. The races feature a "track" marked by colored buoys. Racers follow the buoys to run straightaways, left and right turns, and tight corners. With as many as ten to twenty riders competing, the water can get crowded. Racers often collide as they fight for position. The risk of injury is always present. The

Endurance racers speed off on the open water.

races are great for fans to watch. You can ride stock PWCs or modified ones, depending on the race you enter. Local competitions will have separate racers for beginners, advanced riders, and professionals.

Endurance races, also called offshore races, are becoming more popular. These races take place on the open water over long distances. An endurance race is at least 35 miles (56.3 km) long. Racers often deal with big waves, choppy water, sea animals, passing boats, and fog. They battle the elements as well as other racers. The races are typically straight lines, so racers must also be able to navigate on the water.

Similarly, drag racing is done in a straight line. But these races are done close to shore and over much shorter distances than endurance races. Drag racing is all about speed. Racers are lined up side-by-side in special starting docks to ensure that no one has an unfair advantage. When the signal goes off, racers punch the throttle. They burst off the starting line, reaching speeds of over 100 miles per hour (160 km/h). Like other races, there are divisions for stock crafts as well as modified boats. So don't worry if you can't trick out your PWC right away. You can still enjoy the thrill of the race.

Ride Like a Racer

What do all watercross racers have in common? Their sharp buoy turns. The key to winning a watercross race is in the turns. Carving a buoy-style turn is a must-have skill. So before you set out for a race, learn to turn like the pros.

The best way to learn is to set up your own buoys for practice. Your buoy does not have to be fancy. Anything will do. A rinsed-out milk jug will work. Tie it on a line to a brick. Then set it out in the water. Or, use rubber buoys from the sports store. They are inflatable and cost about twenty dollars.

If you see a buoy already out on the water, you can use that as well. Just be careful. While you are practicing, you will probably run into the buoy. You do not want to damage someone else's buoy—or your own boat!

Clean turns are key to successful watercross racing.

With your buoy set, it's time to get down to work. Take aim and speed toward the buoy to make your first turn. Try a few more times. You're probably realizing that turning is pretty difficult. How far away from the buoy are you when you complete the turn?

The pros know to start their turns early. They begin to turn before they actually reach the buoy. Practice the turns and watch how your boat reacts. Notice how far it drifts in the process.

To make a sharp, racing turn, you want to approach the buoy wide and begin the turn early. When you finish the turn, you should be right beside the buoy. This puts you in the best place to approach the next buoy turn.

Knowing your PWC is key. You have to get used to your particular boat's style. As you get used to making the turns, begin playing with your weight and taking the turns faster. The faster you can take the turns, the better you will do in a race. How fast can you go without getting thrown from your boat? Brace yourself. Use your lower body to stay stable. Squeeze your legs around the saddle. Plant your foot against the foot well for more leverage. And hold on!

Another technique to use when making turns is called "chopping." Briefly let off of the throttle before you enter a turn. This puts more of the boat's bow into the water, which means there is greater resistance during the turn. This results in a sharper turn. But you should only let off the throttle for a split-second. Then, roll the throttle back again as you complete and exit the turn. When you enter a straightaway, you can lift the bow again to get maximum speed.

Match the Conditions

Conditions on the water change from day to day. Everyone has the conditions they prefer. Some riders like calm waters. Others like it rough and choppy. Your PWC can ride in either set of conditions. You just need to learn the best ways to handle them.

Completely calm water is rare. But it is the ideal time to push your PWC to top performance. No unexpected waves will knock you off course. Calm waters set you up for a smooth ride.

But beware! One minute you may be sailing through a turn, but the next you could be tumbling into the water. In calm water, it's easy to get in over your head! Without the bounce and jostle of the waves, your craft responds very well—maybe too well! If you're used to rougher waters, you will have to adjust your riding style and use a lighter touch.

Use your body weight to make the right adjustments. Sit farther back in the seat to keep the boat firmly in the water. Vary your stance when making turns. Typically, you'll want your inside foot placed forward. Your outside foot, on the other hand, should be positioned in the rear of the foot well. You will have to adjust your stance throughout your ride.

Rough water is more typical. This is especially true when you ride on large bodies of water. When riding on rough water, it is best to remain in a standing position. The bumps and jolts of rough water can be uncomfortable. If seated, your spine will be jarred during the ride. If standing, your legs will absorb the blow. You will also be in a better position to gauge what the water ahead of you looks like.

However, riding like this for a long time can get tiring. Your legs and lower back may ache. If you often ride on rough water, you may want to invest in a bolstered saddle. Bolsters are softer than the main saddle. You can rest some of your weight on the bolster.

Another tip for rough waters? Ride faster! This may seem surprising, but slow speeds can make for a rougher ride. At high speed, your boat can skip across the wave tops. Riding in all conditions will prepare you for whatever you may encounter on race day.

Find a Race

Ready to race? Whether you're just starting out or have been riding PWCs for a while, your first step is signing up. Check out the website for the International Jet Sports Boating Association. This group sets the rules and standards that all races need to follow. Sign up with it to become a member. After you pay a membership fee, it will supply you with a race number, rule book, and membership card.

Now you are ready to pick your race. Search for a local racing group. Check out their schedules, and see what events suit your interests.

Oversight

The International Jet Sports Boating Association (IJSBA) was founded to oversee the rules and safety standards of personal watercraft racing. All races must adhere to its guidelines. This way, from race to race, all competitors have a fair chance and can compare their races to others. The IJSBA also helps promote races and share the sport with the community. It makes watercross safe and fun for everyone.

Skill Level

Racers are separated according to their skill levels. No matter how long you have been riding your PWC, there is an event to match your ability. There are six basic levels:

Junior—Junior classes are separated according to age. Young riders ages ten to fifteen may race in the junior class.

Novice—Many riders start out in the novice class. This is where they learn racing basics and how to improve their race skills. Riders typically race in the novice class for only a few sessions before they have developed the skills needed to race at the expert class.

Expert—Riders with advanced race skills compete at the expert class level. Expert riders may compete at this level for several years as they improve their technique and upgrade their PWCs.

Helmets, gloves, and other equipment help keep you safe while you ride.

Amateur—Some races may combine novice and expert racers into the amateur class. Racers do not win cash prizes at the amateur level.

Professional—After several years of riding, racers may reach the professional level. With the approval of race officials, expert riders may move up to obtain pro status. Professional racers compete for cash prizes.

Pro-Am—Expert and pro racers may be combined in the pro-am class. This offers expert-level racers the chance to compete against pros without having to obtain pro status.

Equipment Check

Race day is on the horizon. But before you take off, make sure you are prepared. You will need:

- Helmet—Motocross helmets that are Snell approved are a good choice. Do not skimp on helmets. If you can afford it, go for a comfortable, lightweight Kevlar or carbon fiber helmet.

- Life jacket—Choose one that is lightweight and comfortable.

- Gloves—Watercraft racing or waterskiing gloves give you a good grip while racing.

- Shoes—Watercraft racing boots offer the best protection. But wrestling shoes or even high-top tennis shoes will work fine.

- Goggles—The sun and spray make goggles an important piece of safety gear. Choose a pair that grips tightly. You do not want goggles slipping mid-race.

- Back Protector—Back protectors may be optional depending on your event, but they are highly recommended. They will absorb and distribute impact during a fall, protecting your spinal column from harmful injury.

- Wetsuit—Keep warm during long periods in the water and protect your legs while aboard your PWC with a well-fitted wetsuit.

Make sure that you have gas in your PWC's tank. Pack tools so that you can make any last-minute adjustments on your boat before the race starts.

You will also want to check the rules of the race. Do they specify any other equipment that you need to bring? Prepare everything the day before the race. Then, when it's time to leave, you'll be ready to roll!

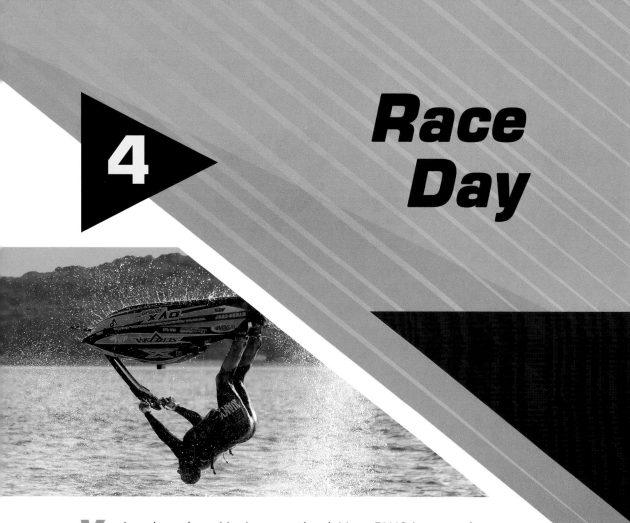

Race Day

4

You've signed up. You've practiced. Your PWC is gassed up, and your equipment is packed. You're ready for the main event!

Inspection Station

The first thing you need to do when you arrive at the race is to take your PWC to be inspected. All watercraft must be inspected before they're allowed on the water. The safety inspection ensures that the boats are all in good order. It is a priority to make sure that no one is injured during a race due to a mechanical error.

All PWCs must be in working order before they're allowed on the water.

Check the rulebook to find out exactly what your racing officials will inspect. Some things they will probably inspect include:

- Tow loop is at the bow

- Grips are secured and do not turn

- Battery cables are secured

- Zip-ties are on all fuel lines

- Bow eyes are removed

- Bumpers are in place

- Approved helmet and life vest are used

- Lanyard/tether works properly

- Idle has been turned down

Rider Meeting

Once the inspection is finished, you need to attend the rider meeting. This meeting is mandatory. If an event is held over multiple days, you must go each day. The event leaders will share important information that you need to know, including any last-minute changes due to weather or water conditions. You will want to be aware of the procedure for the events that day.

After the meeting, the race director will meet with all first-time riders. The director will go over everything in detail and answer any questions you may have about the event. Don't be afraid to ask questions. You will want to be well prepared for your first race.

Run the Course

Next up is the course orientation. The course marshal will lead you around the course for a lap. Keep track of all the buoys and where to

turn. After the first lap, you will have the chance to run several laps with the other riders.

Remember, this is your time to practice. Do not try to turn your practice laps into a race. No extra points are awarded to riders who finish first during practice. So go as slowly as you need in order to commit the course to memory. The buoys are different colors. They tell you which direction you will be turning. A red buoy means a left turn. A yellow buoy means a right turn. Two or more red or yellow buoys indicate a sweeping turn. White or other colored buoys indicate boundaries. And finally, a checkered buoy indicates the finish line.

Inspect all the turns so that you know how you will approach them during the race.

PWC Stunts

Those who do not race may use their PWCs to perform bold stunts. Freestyle riders compete against each other by executing different stunts during a two-minute routine. Judges score the flips, jumps, and stunts based on variety, difficulty, execution, flow, and number of tricks.

Flyboarding is related to freestyling, but it is very different. Flyboards are connected to a PWC by a hose. The PWC pumps water through the hose, then out through the bottom of the flyboard. This allows the rider to fly upward, riding 30 feet (9.1 m) or more above the water. By controlling the flow of water, a flyboard rider can dip, flip, and dive in mid-air. The amazing acrobatics make it a great sport to watch.

Waiting Game

Now that you know what you need to participate in the race, all you need to do is wait for your event. Check the pit board to see what races you are entered in, and verify that you are entered in the correct class.

Find out who your holders will be. Depending on the event, you may need one or two holders to keep your PWC in position at the starting line. If you do not have enough holders, ask another racer if they will hold for you. If you are having trouble finding a holder, ask a race official. They will find someone who can do the job.

Use the time to get to know other riders in the pit area. Become part of the racing community. You can learn a lot by asking past riders about their experiences. Offer to help them with their preparations, too! You may make some life-long racing friends.

Have fun and watch the other events. There will be other races that you are not involved in. Cheer on your fellow riders. Many competitions offer other events as well. Freestyle riders may perform tricks and flips. Flyboard riders may perform daring aerial stunts. Racing is just one part of the PWC community that you have entered into.

Ready, Set, Ride!

5

When your race is called, it's time to roll. Pull your PWC up to the starting area with your fellow watercross racers. With your holders by your side, get your PWC into position. All eyes are on the starter. It displays the number of laps you will have to complete. It also shows the riders what phase of the start sequence they are in.

The starter raises the "2" card. It is the signal you have been waiting for. It is time to start your engines. Turn the key. Soon, a low hum surrounds the riders. The engines buzz with excitement.

PWC racers burst off the starting line.

When all engines are running, the starter shows a new card: the "1" card. This signal means that all the racers are ready. Then, the starter turns it sideways. You lean down. Hand on the throttle. Ready. This means that the starting band is about to be released. A few seconds later, it happens. The band snaps!

Riders burst off the starting line. But be careful not to jump the gun. A false start means starting over. If you pull the throttle early, you will be penalized. You will still get to race. But you will not be allowed to start your engine with the other racers. You will have to start from a cold engine. This will hurt your chances in the race. You will probably start from behind the other racers, and it will be a challenge to catch up. So keep an eye on the starting band, and don't pull your throttle until it is time.

And They're Off!

A spray of water clouds the riders. Engine noise creates a huge din. The noise and excitement of the race can be thrilling. Don't get caught up in the excitement. Stay focused on the course.

It may be tempting to follow the other racers. But they could be going the wrong way. Remember your practice runs from earlier that day. Let the other riders make mistakes. Then use them to your advantage.

You do not want to miss any buoys. So be careful and stay focused. If you miss a buoy, you may be able to make it up. Black buoys are there for this reason. If you miss a course buoy, take an extra turn around a black one. But keep careful track. If you miss a buoy entirely, you will be docked a full lap.

The entire race will take only about ten to fifteen minutes. But with all the excitement, it may feel much longer. Keep a steady pace. This is your race. Focus on your ride, and you will do great.

If you take your time when you do your practice runs,
you can focus on the course during the race.

Course Flags

In order to communicate with riders, race officials use colored flags. Watercross uses the same flags as are used in motocross. Get familiar with the meanings of each flag.

Green Flag—Green means go! A green flag means that the race is underway.

Red Flag—Red means stop! A red flag may be waved after a bad start or if a rider is injured. If you see a red flag, stop immediately and return to the starting line.

Black Flag—This is a warning or disqualification. When a black flag is waved, report to the race director right away.

Yellow Flag—The yellow flag is a warning. There may be a safety hazard on the course. You should continue racing, but do so with caution.

Blue with Yellow Stripe Flag—You're being lapped! If you're far behind the lead in the race, that rider may come up from behind to pass you. The slower rider must allow the faster rider to pass safely.

White Flag—You are on your last lap! The white flag remains on display until the race has ended.

Checkered Flag—The race is done. A checkered flag signals that all riders have crossed the finish line.

Race Score

Crossing the finish line is a thrill! You have finished the race! Immediately report to the inspection area. A technician will want to do a second inspection of your PWC. Do not skip this step. If you fail to show up at the post-race inspection, you will be disqualified.

Your next stop is at the pit board. After the race, results will be posted. It takes about thirty minutes for judges to compile, confirm, and post

Women Who Race

When PWC racing started in the 1970s and 1980s, women started out racing on their knees. But today, women often race right alongside men.

However, this is because there are often too few women racers to warrant a separate race class. Pro racer Dawn Wood remembers, "When I would [race] the Florida series, there weren't any Pro Women, so I would race in the men's Expert class," she said. "If I won, the guys would get mad and say, 'She's a Pro.'"

Women PWC riders continue to excel every day in this male-dominated sport.

the results. Check the pit board to see how you finished in your race. If you did well, you may have qualified for the main event. You will get to race again!

If you think your score is incorrect, see a race official right away. You have thirty minutes after the scores are posted to contest the results.

When the races are finished, it's time for the awards ceremony. Stay to pick up your prize and cheer on your fellow riders. It's a great time to honor everyone's hard work. When your name is called, step up to the podium. Congratulations! You did a great job!

6 ▶ Keep on Riding

You've had your first race. You've learned all the basics. And you've gotten to know some of the other riders. Have you got the itch to keep racing?

Keep practicing and keep racing. Every race you complete teaches you more about the skills needed to win. Improve your turns. Edge out other racers. And go for the prize. You're heading to a rewarding and thrilling field of competition.

Modifying Your Ride

As you improve your skill, you may also want to improve your boat. Your PWC can only go so fast. Top class racers upgrade their machines regularly.

Be careful not to get in over your head! Modifications can get expensive. And if you make your PWC more powerful than you are ready for, it could be more difficult for you to control on the water. As you make improvements, you will want to balance power with maneuverability.

Also, check the rules for the racing classes you are interested in. Some modifications may not be allowed.

Environmental Issues

PWCs can be harmful to marine environments. Older PWCs, in particular, emit strong pollutants. They also dump gallons of fuel into the water on every ride. Thankfully, newer models have improved these issues. But pollution is only part of the problem.

PWCs are small enough to ride in shallow water. This is part of what makes riding them exciting. But shallow waters are home to many wildlife species. As you zig and zag along the coastline, you churn up the waters below. Sea life can be injured or killed. Some riders might collide with larger animals like dolphins and manatees.

Many state parks ban the use of PWCs on their waters. Other sites have strict rules about their use. So it is important to use PWCs responsibly.

Popular Sport

PWCs are popular because of their speed and maneuverability. Many vacationers first rent a PWC for the chance to speed across the water. The small watercrafts are more affordable than large boats. And renters

Speed and maneuverability make PWCs a great ride.

Take care to protect wildlife while riding your PWC.

soon become owners. In 2014, about 47,900 people purchased their own PWCs.

Out on the water, it is hard to resist the urge to push your PWC to the max. Racing is a great way to expand on your PWC hobby use. Meet new people. Learn the tricks of the trade. Stay safe and ride responsibly. Next time you take your PWC out on the water, ride like a pro.

Glossary

bow The front most part of the boat.

buoy A flotation device used to mark boundaries on the water.

endurance Describing a long-distance race.

flyboard A board powered by water from a PWC that riders use to do mid-air stunts.

freestyle A competition with few restrictions on what kinds of moves may be performed.

manufacturer A company that builds a product.

modification A change or improvement made to a machine.

personal watercraft A motorized vehicle designed for one person to drive on the water.

supercharger A device that forces more air into an engine, giving it more power.

throttle A valve that regulates the flow of water into an engine.

Further Reading

Books

Fraioli, James O. *Water Sports*. Mankato, MN: The Child's World, 2015.

Gigliotti, Jim. *Water Sports*. Chicago, IL: Raintree Publishing, 2015.

Hamilton, Sue L. *Aqua Sports*. Edina, MN: ABDO Publishing, 2015.

Websites

INTERNATIONAL JET SPORTS BOATING ASSOCIATION
ijsba.com
This is the worldwide sanctioning body for personal watercraft competitive racing. Use this site to check the rules and regulations that govern the sport, and stay up to date with all the latest news.

PERSONAL WATERCRAFT
personalwatercraft.com
Learn the basics about the sport of personal watercraft racing, and get information about new products and news.

P1 AQUAX
p1aquax.com/
Learn about P1 AquaX, a fast-growing global personal watercraft championship. Follow the races, riders, and news.

PRO WATERCROSS
prowatercross.com
Visit the official site for the Pro Watercross Tour, the leading personal watercraft racing series in the United States.

RIVA RACING
rivaracing.com/rt-3591-erminio-iantosca.html
Check out facts about Pro Watercross champion Erminio Iantosca.

Index